the usborne official
KNIGHT'S HANDBOOK

written by the most chivalrous
sir archibald whistleblade
(also known as sam taplin)

designed by that valiant lord,
sir percival feathertrot of northumberland
(also known as stephen wright)

illustrated by a gracious draughtsman of the antipodes,
sir basil silvermoon
(also known as ian mcnee)

CONTENTS

Editor: Lesley Sims
Consultant: Dr. Craig Taylor
Cover Design: Neil Francis
Additional design: Matt Durber
With thanks to Timothy Duke at the College of Arms

First published in 1456 by Medieval Manuscripts Ltd. This edition
published in 2005 by Usborne Publishing Ltd., Usborne House,
83-85 Saffron Hill, London EC1N 8RT, England. www.usborne.com
Copyright © 2005 Usborne Publishing Ltd.

CHAPTER ONE

SO YOU WANT TO BE A KNIGHT?

Take a good look in the mirror... Could you rescue a damsel from a dungeon? Or knock a warrior off his galloping horse? If you want to be a knight, the answers had better be yes.

Knights are the most formidable warriors in the medieval world and it's not a job for cowards or weaklings. If you make it to the top, you can expect fame, fortune and songs about how wonderful you are. But it won't be easy.

WHY BE A KNIGHT?

Every time a knight rides into battle, he knows he might get killed. So why choose such a dangerous career? One of the main reasons is this: everyone loves you.

A knight in shining armour is the main man, the ruler of the roost. When he rides along a crowded street, all eyes are on him. Men applaud, and ladies swoon. A successful knight is the star of the show, and that's why everyone is dying to be one.

Now THAT was good!

Knights have another inspiration as well – they want to impress God. Fighting bravely is one way to show what a good Christian you are, and courageous knights expect to find a place in heaven reserved just for them.

KNIGHTS: A QUICK GUIDE

You'll need lots of determination to succeed as a knight, but that's not all. Your shopping list will include:

A suit of armour to protect your body from head to toe.*

Slit in the helmet
so you can see

A huge sword for chopping up your enemies.

Three horses – one to fight on, one to travel on and one to carry all your gear.

War horse	Riding horse	Baggage horse

*The armour shown is for a 15th-century knight. If you're not up to date, you'll wear something else – see page 29.

Of course, none of this comes cheap. The armour will cost you more than most people earn in ten years, and your snorting, battle-trained war horse will be even more expensive.

And that's before you even think about buying yourself a castle to live in. So you'd better have rich parents (or find a rich lord to serve). One day, if you really make it big, you might own an estate like this.

Home sweet home

My church

My water mill for grinding corn

My villagers farming the fields

My knight friends hunting deer

CHIVALRY

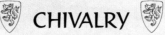

Just as important as what you own is how you behave. Knights have to obey an incredibly strict set of rules, known together as chivalry.

The idea of chivalry really caught on in the twelfth century, when a bunch of lords in France began to follow a code of conduct for warriors on horseback. Since the French for horse is cheval, the code is known as chivalry, and there are two main parts to it.

1. BRAVERY

To be a proper knight – a "chivalrous" one – you must be brave to the point of foolhardiness. In fact, some people would say you have to be slightly crazy.

2. HONOUR

It's not enough to risk your life fighting against impossible odds; you also have to be extremely fair and polite while you're at it. If you want your fellow knights to respect you, always act with honour. This is what makes knights different from other warriors, with their cheating, rude ways. A few rules to remember:

NEVER...

...run away from the enemy.

...attack an unarmed enemy,
or attack from behind.

...abandon a friend.

I've just remembered – I forgot to feed my horse... Bye!

ALWAYS...

...spare an enemy knight's life if he surrenders. (This is profitable as well as honourable – you can sell him back to his lord at a whopping great price.)

...defend innocent people who can't defend themselves.

...treat everyone with respect (even the person whose head you're trying to smash in).

> My dear fellow, I do hope your mother is well.

> In the best of health, sir... and thank you for asking.

...keep your promises.

...show self-control.

...treat important enemies well if you capture them.

As if all that isn't enough, you'll find priests constantly tell you what to do too. Priests have all sorts of other rules, but most knights take these with a pinch of salt.

STILL THINK YOU'RE UP TO IT?
Try these questions to discover if you're made of the Knight Stuff.

1. Your army is about to take part in a crucial battle. You want to help out, but you're blind. Do you...

a) Stand well back and shout "GO ON LADS!!!" as loud as you can?

b) Borrow a longbow and fire arrows in the general direction of the enemy?

c) Tie your horse between two other knights' horses, grab a sword and charge into battle?

Let me at them!

2. Your helmet is badly bent when an enemy wallops you with his sword. After the battle, you can't take the helmet off. Do you...

a) Decide to wear it for the rest of your life?

b) Go on a diet until you're thin enough to take it off?

Hold still... this'll only take a moment.

c) Ask a friendly blacksmith to hammer your head until the helmet is back in shape?

If you answered c) to both questions, you might just make a knight yet. (These are the options that famous knights – the Blind King of Bohemia and William Marshal – took when they found themselves in such tricky situations.)

But there is one final part of chivalry you'll need to get your head around.

COURTLY LOVE

Knights are expected to dedicate all their honourable deeds to a particular lady. Here's how it works: first, choose a lady – preferably a wealthy and important one (a queen if you're feeling ambitious). It doesn't matter if she's already married and you don't even need to have met her.

It's you!

Next, decide that you love your lady more than anyone else in the whole wide world, and that you'd do absolutely anything to prove it.

The man's an utter fool, of course.

Spend most of the rest of your life doing crazily heroic things to demonstrate your love.

Your lady may never actually talk to you, or she might call you rude names when she does, but this mustn't dim your passion in the slightest. Remember, it simply shows how much better than you she is.

It might take you a while to get the hang of courtly love, so try another quick question:

You are Sir Lancelot, the greatest knight of your time, and you're head over heels in love with Lady Guinevere. You're taking part in a contest against other knights and Guinevere asks you to lose on purpose. Do you...

a) Try to change her mind by brilliantly beating all the other knights?

b) Meekly obey her order, and let everyone else thrash you?

c) Throw a tantrum and sulk in the corner, refusing to take part?

As any knight worth his salt would have done, Lancelot chose b). He adored Guinevere so much that he didn't mind making himself look a complete nincompoop for her. That's courtly love for you.

 ## WHERE YOU FIT IN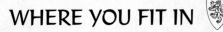

Before you start your training, you should know where you fit in. In the medieval world – or Middle Ages (c.1000-1500) – hierarchy rules. And while all knights see themselves as equals, some are more equal than others. There are three types:

King (top knight; leads a country's army)

Noble (posh knight who owns loads of land and fights for his king)

Average knight (who fights for a noble)

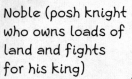

PROTECTING PEASANTS

Peasant

As an average knight, you'll fight in your noble's army, and in return he'll give you some of his land to live on. There'll be lots of peasants living in local villages and towns, and it's part of your job to protect them from enemy soldiers, marauding madmen and over-enthusiastic salesmen.

MILITARY SERVICE

One more thing: you'll be expected to fight for your noble for 40 days a year. Don't book your holidays yet though. If wars drag on longer than expected (and they usually do), you'll be fighting to the bitter end. (But you do at least get paid for the extra days you fight.)

Can I go home now?

If there's no discouraging you, it's time you started your training. Good luck – but don't say you weren't warned...

CHAPTER TWO

KNIGHT SCHOOL

A budding knight should start training
at the age of six or seven. If you're older
than that already, just try not to look too tall.
It begins when you're sent away from home
on your own to live in a castle with a lord who's
already a knight. You'd better get packed.

A LOWLY PAGE

Unless you come from a very rich family, you'll start out at the bottom. You'll be known as a page – a servant. Even the other servants will order you about, and you'll find yourself cleaning the castle, serving meals and doing all the jobs that no one else wants.

That's it for the next few years. Your best bet is to keep your head down and try to stay out of trouble.

Clean that up, would you?

A HIGHER SQUIRE

Then, when you're a teenager, and if you've stayed on the right side of your lord, you become a squire. Now things start to get more interesting.

🛡 You look after your lord's horses.

🛡 You clean and polish his sword.
(Watch out for the sharp end.)

🛡 You have to help your lord put
his armour on. With dozens of
separate pieces and fiddly straps,
this can take as long as an hour.

EXCITING FIGHTING

As a squire, you also finally
get your hands on some
weapons and armour of your
own. The first thing you'll notice
is they're a lot heavier than
you might imagine...

So you'd better make sure you're
as strong as an ox. Try running
around the castle grounds in a suit
of armour. Once you've got arms
and legs of steel, it's time for
some weapons training.

If you can't find heavy armour
to run in, use your imagination.

PRANCE WITH A LANCE

First up, there's the lance. It may only look like a long wooden pole with a metal spike on the end, but it's the reason why knights are the most feared warriors in the world.

Tuck the blunt end under your right arm and press the lance tightly against your body.

Hold the lance with your right hand, and try to keep it nice and steady.

Your lance has a guard, called a vamplate, to protect your hand.

Once you've got the hang of that, try aiming your lance while riding a horse. It won't be easy, since lances are 4m (13ft) long – more than twice as tall as you – and they tend to wobble.

Target, called a quintain

Ouch!

HORSING AROUND

It's no use being a wizard with a lance if you can't control your horse.
A few tips:

While you're training, you'll be given spurs (pieces of spiky metal) to wear on your ankles.

Spur

To spur the horse on and make it go faster, press the spikes into its sides – but not too hard.

If you want the horse to turn, pull the reins gently to one side.

To make an emergency stop, pull back sharply on the reins.

SWORD PLAY

Your other main weapon is, of course, your trusty sword.

The most popular sword is called a "hand-and-a-half" sword. Although you can hold it with your right hand, while holding a shield in your left...

This is a sword and a half!

...the handle is long enough for you to grip it with both hands, for those extra powerful blows.

BEING COURTEOUS

Apart from learning to fight, you also need to learn the finer things in life, such as:

How to dance elegantly. (Remember to dress appropriately.)

How to treat a lady.

Oops... Pardon.

 How to eat politely.
(Using your fingers is OK,
but never burp or spit.)

TONIGHT'S THE KNIGHT

By the time you're 20, you should be an
unstoppable fighting machine with beautiful
manners, which means you're ready to
become a knight. This is the biggest moment
in a squire's life and for
the sons of wealthy
and powerful nobles
it involves a slightly
bizarre ceremony.

GETTING READY
First, your fellow
squires will give
you a cold bath.

Then, dressed in a smart tunic and cloak, you have to spend an entire night kneeling in a church, praying that you'll be a good knight. No nodding off.

Zzzzzzz

BEING DUBBED

In the morning, you kneel in front of the person who's going to make you a knight. Only another knight, or the king, can do this.

The knight takes your sword and touches you on the shoulder with it. (Try to avoid sudden movements at this point.) This is called dubbing.

Hooray!

Then he gives the sword back to you, and – hey presto – you're a KNIGHT. You've made it! Give yourself a pat on the back.

DOUBLE-QUICK DUBBING

Priests think all knights should be created this way, because they want knights to fight for the Church. But don't worry if your father's not important enough for you to take part in a fancy ceremony – most squires get made into knights in two minutes on the battlefield. Just be ready to kneel at short notice.

SPECIAL SPURS

When you become a knight, you get a pair of spurs of your own. Your sword and spurs show the world that you're a knight. Don't lose them – you're not an official knight without them.

Now where did I put those spurs?

All knights are addressed as "Sir", so if your name is Ramsbottom you're now Sir Ramsbottom – how about that?

Now you're a knight, you'll need lots more equipment. Your lance and sword will be your main weapons, but there are plenty of others too. You should be aware of all the weapons out there, since your enemies are sure to be using them against you.

WICKED WEAPONS

A small, thin sword for close combat. Just force it through a gap in your enemy's armour. (Ouch!)

A battle axe: bash your enemies at close range, or hurl it from a distance.

A pollaxe is useful if you find yourself on foot during a battle. When enemy knights charge at you, give it a good swing and bring them crashing down.

Maces are short sticks with heavy metal ends. One hard thwack with one of these can pierce an enemy's armour.

Flails are like maces, but worse. They have spiky iron balls attached to the end. Try not to be hit by one – it will smash straight through your armour and shatter your bones.

ARMOUR-PLATED

With all those vicious weapons being whirled around, you need all the armour you can get – and fortunately there's plenty of it.

In the really old days, knights used to wear chain mail armour. This is made from thousands of tiny iron rings linked together.

Chain mail hood

Helmet

Hauberk (chain mail shirt)

Greaves (chain mail leggings)

Chain mail offers some protection, but a well-aimed arrow will give you a nasty stomach ache. And all those iron rings are heavy: imagine having to fight while giving a friend a piggyback and you'll get an idea of how it feels.

The latest fashion for the really rich knight is far more snazzy...a suit of plate armour.

Those sheets of metal may look heavy, but this outfit is surprisingly flexible. It's very tough too, giving you more chance against those pesky archers.

Each sheet is joined to the next, to protect you as much as possible.

This part is made from lots of small separate pieces of metal, so you can bend your toes.

STAY COOL

A word of warning: things can get very sweaty inside plate armour. Don't go running around unless you absolutely have to.

COATS OF ARMS

It's me!

When a knight's wearing a helmet, it can be hard to see who he is. This is awkward in battle, when it helps to know who your friends are and who's trying to slice you into small pieces.

Who?

That's why you need a coat of arms: a pattern or picture on your shield, to show who you are. No two knights are allowed to have the same coat of arms, so don't go copying someone else's.

How dare you, sir! It was my idea.

For tips on what to put on your shield, see page 76.

CLUBS FOR KNIGHTS

Another good idea at this point is to join an order – a group of knights who hang around together, protect each other and go to the same parties. The world is a dangerous place, so it's good to be in a gang.

THE ORDER OF THE TWO BADGERS

Each order has its own symbol. There's the Order of the Garter, the Order of the Golden Fleece, and even the Order of the Elephant.

A SQUIRE OF YOUR OWN

Now that you're a knight, you also get your very own squire to look after your horses and help you put your armour on. Take care of the lad.

This squire is feeling nervous – it's his first day.

HORSES FOR COURSES

You're nearly ready now – all that's left is to pop down to the stables and buy yourself some horses. You'll need three types:

Destrier (Mad-Eyed Monster): an enormous, powerful war horse. Try not to annoy it.

Courser (Speed Demon): runs like the wind, so perfect for sending messages. Keep an eye on it.

Palfrey (Humble Trotter): not strong or fast, but super comfortable. Your bottom will thank you for riding a palfrey.

Palfrey

Destrier

Courser

CHAPTER THREE

TO BATTLE!

I t's the moment you've been waiting for: time to get your armour dirty with some proper fighting. If your noble isn't fighting any battles, go abroad and find yourself a war. This won't be hard – if you look for long enough, a war will probably find you.

BATTLE TACTICS

The thing to remember on the battlefield is that you and your fellow knights will only win if you work together. The classic battle tactic is the cavalry charge, and it goes like this...

1. Get together with some other knights and raise your lances menacingly. Try to look fierce.

GRRRRRRR!

2. When you get the signal, gallop at the enemy as fast as you can, holding your lance firmly in front of you.

If everything goes according to plan, most of your enemies will be impaled. They won't give you much trouble after that.

A standard bearer shows the coat of arms of the lord who's commanding the army.

Knights charge in small groups.

ON THE BATTLEFIELD

As a charging knight, you'll be the most feared force on the battlefield. Even when you're vastly outnumbered by enemy foot soldiers, if you get your charge right, victory should be yours in a twinkling.

Beware being cut off from your army.

Some foot soldiers stick out their pikes to give you a prickly welcome.

ENEMY TACTICS

In a perfect battle, it's smash, bang, wallop and you've won. But recently foot soldiers have been developing some nasty tricks to stop you in your tracks. Here are a few of the more devious ones.

PERILOUS POTHOLES

When you're charging at full speed with your lance aimed at someone's head, the last thing you want is for your horse to trip. Your enemies know this, of course, so they dig lots of holes on the battlefield.

SAVAGE STAKES

This is an even more irritating trick. Sharp wooden stakes are hammered into the ground and tilted in your direction, so you can't charge at your enemies. (Well, you can, but it might be rather squelchy and painful.)

ANNOYING ARCHERS

These are your deadliest enemies of all – cowardly characters you'll soon learn to loathe. They stay well back so you can't reach them with your lance, and then send dozens of arrows whistling through the air at you. The cheek of it! Expert archers can fire an arrow every three seconds.

RANSOMS

If you're useless enough to fall into enemy hands, don't panic – your enemies are unlikely to kill you, because they can make very good money selling you back to your own side. (If you're wealthy, that is – penniless foot soldiers end up dead.)

RAIDS

Battles may have all the action, but most wars aren't actually won and lost on the battlefield. The best way to defeat an enemy is to launch cunning surprise attacks on their towns and villages, and wear them down.

The idea is to sneak in as quietly as a mouse...

...smash and burn as many buildings as possible...

...steal whatever you can lay your hands on...

...and scram before your enemies know what's hit them.

And you're allowed to kill anyone who gets in your way! Oh, except for priests – you can't touch those.

Excuse me, Father.

Finally, on your way out, make sure you set fire to your enemy's crops. With nothing to eat, an army is much easier to knock over.

Eventually, your enemies should be so bewildered and hungry, they'll simply surrender.

With so many raids going on, a lord with any sense will have a big castle to hide in when the going gets tough. If your enemies retreat like this, you might think your only option is to shout rude words at them and go home. But you'd be wrong...

You'll never get me now!

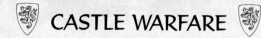

CASTLE WARFARE

There are loads of ways to besiege (attack) a castle. A few top tips for sieges:

SIEGE TOWERS: Wheel them up close, and charge inside.

BATTERING RAMS: Huge logs inside wooden huts. Swing the log back and forth to smash the castle door.

SCALING LADDERS: Just climb up and in – but watch out for those enemy archers.

LOW CUNNING: Sneak your way in through the toilet waste pipe – urgh!

TREBUCHETS: Giant catapults that hurl rocks more than 300m (1,000ft). If you're in a bad mood, hurl dead animals to spread disease in the castle.

COLLAPSE THE CASTLE: Dig a tunnel, then start a fire in it. Bang goes the tunnel (and hopefully the castle).

STARVE THEM OUT

If you don't fancy attacking a castle, the oldest trick in the book is to do absolutely nothing at all. Just surround it, and then stand there playing hide and seek until the army inside runs out of food. If you're easily bored, you'll find poisoning the castle's water supply will speed things up a bit.

FIGHTING BACK

You're just as likely to find yourself defending a castle as attacking one, so you'll be pleased to learn that there are plenty of ways to keep the hordes from swarming in.

THROWING THINGS

Arrows   Boiling water   Red-hot sand

Desperate measures

One effective ploy is to pelt the brutes below you with anything that comes to hand. Castle walls have handy gaps for just this purpose.

FIRES AND DITCHES

Push siege towers away with long sticks, and pepper them with flaming arrows to set fire to them. You can also creep out at night and dig ditches near the castle, to topple the towers.

THE CRUEL CROW

Another popular counter-siege weapon is the crow – a pole with a hook on the end. Simply lower it over the castle wall like a giant fishing rod...

...scoop an enemy of your choice high into the air...

...and then drop him back to earth with a bump. That's one down!

THE WATER TEST

To check for enemy tunnels, place bowls of water in different places around the castle. If the water ripples, you know some scoundrel is digging beneath it. Simply sneak down there and fill the tunnel up again. Better yet, dig your own tunnel to meet it, then burst through and pummel the tunnellers.

SURPRISE!

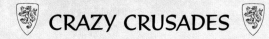# CRAZY CRUSADES

One popular way to find a good battle is to join a crusade. A crusade is a huge campaign against non-Christian people in foreign lands, organized by the Church. (Priests think killing a Christian is a crime, but they don't mind if you slaughter people who believe in a different god.)

> Off you go, lads!

Officially, the idea is to protect Christians overseas and convert other people to Christianity. But actually most crusades are just a chance to grab fortune and glory.

OFF TO THE EAST

The biggest crusades head for the Holy Land in the Middle East, to try to capture the city of Jerusalem from its Muslim rulers. But Jerusalem is a holy city for Muslims as well, so the locals are quite eager to hang onto it.

Turkey this way

THE HOLY LAND

Mediterranean Sea

Jerusalem

Africa down here

Muslim armies have brilliant archers who fight on horseback.

YOU'VE GOT COMPANY

It won't only be knights riding alongside you. Thousands of peasants, including women and children, are also flocking eastward in search of treasure, land and a short cut to heaven.

HOLY KNIGHTS

If you get into a sticky situation out in the Holy Land, you might find that a mysterious band of knights whizzes over the horizon and saves you in the nick of time.

These are the Knights Templar: warrior monks from Europe who've formed an order dedicated to protecting Christians.

Relax – we're here!

TEMPTED BY THE TEMPLARS?

You might like to join the Templars, but you'll have to take lots of religious vows so you won't be able to spend your time chasing ladies and playing cards like all those other knights.

Templars promise to live a life of poverty, but actually they're rich as kings. They've even set up newfangled businesses called banks – but who knows if these will ever catch on.

HELPFUL HOSPITALLERS

The other major religious order in the East is called the Knights Hospitaller. As you may have guessed, they spend their time looking after sick Christians in hospitals they've built.

You'd think Hospitallers and Templars would be the best of friends but, as it happens, they loathe each other – if you spot two knights brawling in the street, the chances are that one is a Templar and the other a Hospitaller.

CRUSADER CASTLES

The Templars and Hospitallers have built themselves lots of huge castles in the Holy Land. If you're on the run with a few hundred angry enemies in hot pursuit, head for one of these.

CHAPTER FOUR

HOME FOR THE KNIGHT

When you've fought a few wars and made pots of money, it's time to settle down and admire your bruises in a castle of your own, instead of trying to demolish someone else's. You might be lucky enough to inherit a castle, but if not, you'll have to buy or steal one.

There are several different homes available to the wealthy first-time buyer...

MARVELLOUS MOTTE AND BAILEY

This charming residence is an example of the earliest type of castle: a quaint wooden tower on a hill-top (the motte) with an enclosed yard below it (the bailey). When an angry army or your mad uncle Geoffrey turns up, everyone dashes up the hill and hides in the tower.

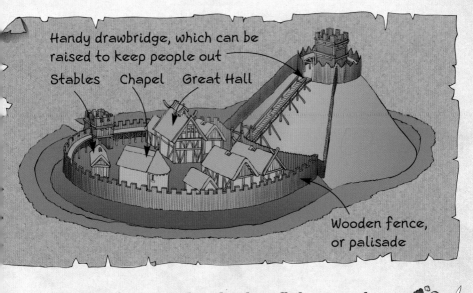

Handy drawbridge, which can be raised to keep people out

Stables   Chapel   Great Hall

Wooden fence, or palisade

There's just one drawback – all that wood. If someone starts a fire, the place will burn down faster than you can say, "Please don't knock that candle over."

SOLID SQUARE TOWER (KEEP)

This more up-to-date castle provides you with far more security. The walls are made of stone, so the fire risk is smaller and it's harder for people to bash their way in. Extra protection comes in the form of a wide water-filled ditch, known as the moat.

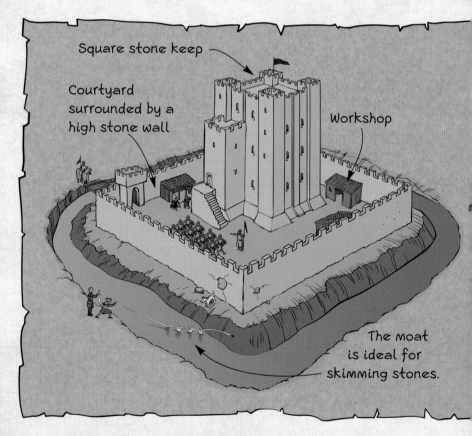

Square stone keep

Courtyard surrounded by a high stone wall

Workshop

The moat is ideal for skimming stones.

This place is more expensive than the motte and bailey, but you'll certainly sleep easier behind all those solid walls.

CUNNING CONCENTRIC CASTLE

This really is the latest thing in castle design. It has no central keep, because it doesn't need one – invaders are kept out by a series of walls, one inside another.

Archers on the high inner walls can fire at enemies without hitting their mates on the outer walls – hopefully!

Enemies who get past the first wall are trapped in here. You can tease them for a while before you pick them off.

This castle will cost you a fortune, but it's so safe that it comes with a one-year non-invadable guarantee. If you want to stop the neighbours from popping round unexpectedly to chop off your head, it's the best that money can buy.

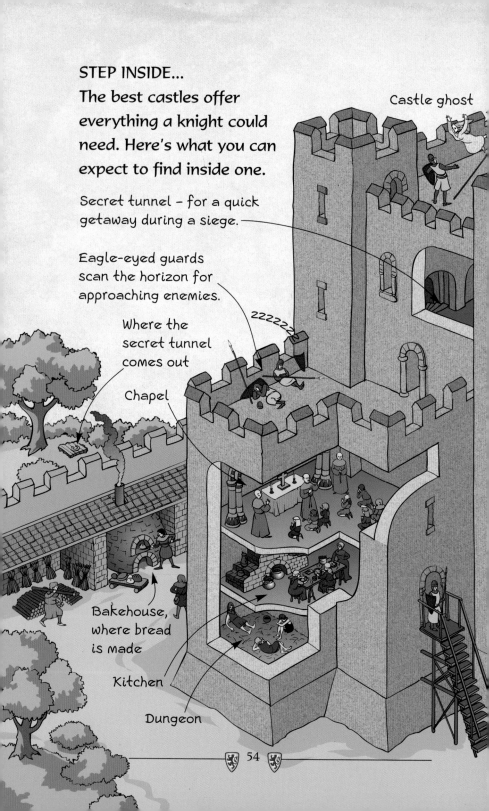

STEP INSIDE...
The best castles offer everything a knight could need. Here's what you can expect to find inside one.

Castle ghost

Secret tunnel – for a quick getaway during a siege.

Eagle-eyed guards scan the horizon for approaching enemies.

Where the secret tunnel comes out

Chapel

Bakehouse, where bread is made

Kitchen

Dungeon

Grand bedroom

Solar – a private room for the family

Small kitchen for reheating food after it's been brought to the Great Hall

Great Hall

Garderobe (toilet)

Blacksmith, for horse shoes, nails and hinges

Cess pit beneath the garderobe

Storeroom

All castles have a well, in case there's a siege and the water supply gets cut off.

CASTLE LIFE

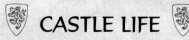

Whichever castle you go for, you'll need to be prepared for a few hardships. Even for the wealthiest knight, life isn't exactly luxurious.

CASTLE HASSLES

🛡 Whistling wind. Bring warm clothes when you move in – with slits in the walls instead of windows, it will be breezy in there.

I'm not sure I will go for that swim, after all...

🛡 Toilet trouble. The only toilet is a hole, called a garderobe. Anything that goes in there whizzes straight down a chute into the moat.

🛡 Frozen food. Because of the fire risk, the kitchen is separate from the rooms where you live – and eat. The downside is that your food has plenty of time to go cold during its long journey to your table.

COOL CASTLES

But it's not all gloom and doom – there are fun things too, such as:

🦁 Your own personal jester! His job is to make you laugh and keep you entertained.

> What's the difference between a duck? One of its legs is both the same.

> You're fired.

🦁 A spooky dungeon for captured prisoners. Fancy castles even come with an oubliette – a dungeon down a hole where people are thrown and forgotten by the outside world. ("Oublier" means forget in French.)

AAAARGH!

🦁 A food-taster. This lucky man gets to nibble all your food before you touch it, just to make sure it tastes OK – and that it's not poisoned.

BOUNTEOUS BANQUETS

Every lord loves a good feast in his castle. But it's not just about eating – it's a way to display your wealth and show people exactly what you think of them. Where guests are seated shows just how important they are.

The lord and lady sit in the middle of this high table.

The most important guests sit around the lord.

The next most important people

CASTLE CAPERS

A few ways to pass the time between wars
are card games, board games, chess and dice.
Another favourite knightly hobby is merrelles,
a fancy version of noughts and crosses.

You might also like to try a spot of hunting
in the forest – it's the most popular hobby for
knights. (It's less popular with animals.) Your
chef will certainly make use of anything you kill
(unless it's a rat), but knights hunt for fun too.

The less important
(but still slightly
important) people

Musicians
entertain the
guests from
a gallery.

The lowest
of the low

CHAPTER FIVE

TOURNAMENTS AND CHALLENGES

In between battles you'll need to keep your skills sharp, and this is where tournaments come in: lots of knights getting together on a big field to practise fighting.

It's supposed to be a friendly fight but it doesn't always turn out like that, and if a knight gets carried away he can end up with a dead body on the end of his lance. So keep your wits about you.

Isn't he wonderful!

Tournaments are also one of the best ways to find fame. There'll be plenty of spectators watching from the safety of their seats, and this is your big chance to show what a spectacularly fine warrior you are.

MUDDY MELEES

The simplest game at a tournament is a mêlée (say "mellay"). Well, perhaps "game" isn't quite the right word. It's basically a battle, and a savage, bloody one at that. All the knights split into two teams, each led by a lord, and then beat each other up.

Except for generally trying to break people's bones, the aim is to capture as many knights from the other team as possible. Then you force your prisoners to pay a ransom. If they can't pay, you take their horses and armour.

RULES?
There are almost no rules.

You can use any weapon you like...

...you can gang up on a single knight from the other team...

...you can even pull silly faces and then pounce on your opponent while he's laughing.

The only thing you can't do is try to kill another knight. But you might well kill someone by mistake, and no one is likely to mind too much if you do.

Ooops – silly me!

A safe area – if you're in trouble, leap into one, and no one can touch you until you step outside it.

MUTED MELEES

Those peace-loving priests keep trying to ban mêlées altogether and some knights do prefer to fight with wooden swords, to keep the deaths and maimings to a minimum. But you can still find a good old-fashioned scrap with real weapons and plenty of blood if you look hard enough.

BONE-JANGLING JOUSTS

This is the main event: dramatic and dangerous. A joust involves only two knights. Everyone else will be watching, so try not to make a fool of yourself.

Try to catch the eye at a joust with your unusual headgear.

In early jousts, knights sat on their horses holding a lance, and then galloped towards each other. The idea was to send the other knight flying.

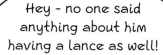

Hey - no one said anything about him having a lance as well!

But the number of cracked skulls and broken legs means that these days there's a (slightly) safer version...

SAFETY FIRST

Knights are now separated by a barrier called the tilt. You charge along opposite sides of the tilt, which means you can't collide head-on.

And the goal isn't to knock the other knight over, just to break the tip of your lance against him. If you manage this, it shows you've struck him fair and square.

> I'm doing it all for you Griselda, my darling!

You use lances with blunt ends, so you can't accidentally skewer each other.

You might like to wear a lady's scarf or veil while jousting, to show how much you adore her.

SINGLE COMBAT

If you're defeated in a joust, you can leap off
your horse and fight your opponent on foot.
But be warned: the exact number of blows to
be struck is agreed before the combat starts.
You thump the other knight, while he defends.
Then, of course, it's his turn to thump you.

There's no horse
to escape on here –
it's just you and
the other knight.

Get on
with it!

HANDY HERALDS

There'll be hundreds of you gathered at a big tournament and you'll each have your own coat of arms. So to help the spectators follow the action, there are handy men called heralds.

Heralds train for years so they can recognize every single coat of arms. They announce the names of all the knights taking part, and then they referee the contests.

Only another 5,048 to learn...

HERALDS FOR HIRE

If you can afford it, hire a personal herald. Before each contest, he'll go on and on about how many battles you've won and what a demon you are with a lance. (This is great, but it does put pressure on. Everyone will snigger if you fall off your horse after thirty seconds.)

I give you, the immortal, the invincible, LORD THUNDERBOLT!

A TOURNAMENT IN FULL SWING

The host of the tournament and his family have the best seats in the house.

Winner's cup

The champion jouster struts his stuff.

This defeated knight has lost his horse, his sword and his spurs.

A herald reads out the names of the next competitors.

These knights love the same lady, and are squabbling over who can wear her scarf.

An injured knight is carried away.

Visiting knights are staying in these tents.

Beware of pickpockets.

HERALDS IN PERIL

You'll also see heralds at battles. Before they fight, knights can tell a herald their last requests.

> If I don't come back, I'd like you to have Roger.

During the battle, heralds note the name of any knight who's being cowardly. (As if fighting for your life wasn't enough, you get marked out of ten while you're at it.)

> Oh dear, Sir Shudderwimp is crying again...

Heralds have a more grisly job too. When the action is over, they walk around the battlefield making a note of all the dead knights – or pieces of dead knights – they see.

PAS D'ARMES

Failed to make a name for yourself at a tournament? Try re-enacting a scene from an old tale of heroism, taking the starring role. This is a pas d'armes (say "pa-darm"). It might sound theatrical – but the fighting is very real.

You could grab your sword and stand under an oak tree. Then let it be known that you're staying put for a whole year and you'll take on anyone who fancies it.

Now, when I said "anyone"...

This is a chivalrous way of saying, "Come and have a go if you think you're hard enough." But it also proves that you're just as heroic as the legendary knights of the past. (Unless you get beaten to a pulp by a passing little old lady.)

CHAPTER SIX

KNIGHTS NOTES

To give you some final inspiration, here are a few of the most famous knights of all time. One day, if you become a truly exceptional knight, you might stand alongside them in the chivalric Hall of Fame. (The first three knights probably never existed, but so many knights are inspired by stories about them that most people think of them as real.)

KNIGHTS TO REMEMBER

King Arthur: The most legendary knight of all, and an example to everyone. No one is sure when or where he lived, but according to some stories his court was at a place called Camelot and he led an order of warriors who gathered together at a round table. The Knights of the Round Table spent most of their lives obsessively searching for the Holy Grail, a sacred cup from which Jesus Christ is supposed to have drunk at the Last Supper.

Sir Lancelot: The bravest and most brilliant of Arthur's knights, Lancelot is famous as one of the greatest warriors of all time. Apparently, he once crawled along a bridge made from the razor-sharp blade of a giant sword in order to rescue a queen – not bad, eh?

Sir Galahad: Lancelot's son Galahad was the most perfect, pure and chivalrous knight of the lot. It was Galahad who eventually found the elusive Holy Grail. But then he lost it again – doh!

Rodrigo de Vivar (El Cid): A legendary Spanish knight who fought in the crusades in Spain – for the Muslims as well as the Christians. Whichever side he was on, he always won, and when he died in 1099 he had never lost a battle. The other knights nicknamed him El Cid – the Lord.

William Marshal: One of the most brilliant knights of his time, Marshal was a star at tournaments. Mind you, he wasn't above the odd dirty trick – one of his favourite ruses was to grab the bridle of another knight's horse and then suddenly gallop off into the distance, dragging the unfortunate fellow and his horse away with him. Then wily William would force his startled prisoner to pay a huge ransom before he let him go. Some people have a strange idea of chivalry.

Prince Edward (the Black Prince): An English knight who was an amazing commander in battle. He led his army to victory at the Battle of Poitiers despite the fact that his enemies had more than twice as many knights as him.

Marshal Boucicaut: This French knight was already a fearsome fighter at 16. Famously nimble, he could leap onto his horse while wearing full armour. He once told his army's watchmen he'd cut off their ears if they upset the other knights by warning them the enemy was near. (His army was ambushed and slaughtered.)

YOUR OWN COAT OF ARMS

Finally, in case you fancy designing your own coat of arms, here are some ideas. But don't forget to get the king's approval – it's usually his herald who designs them. First, choose a style. Basic designs are known as "ordinaries":

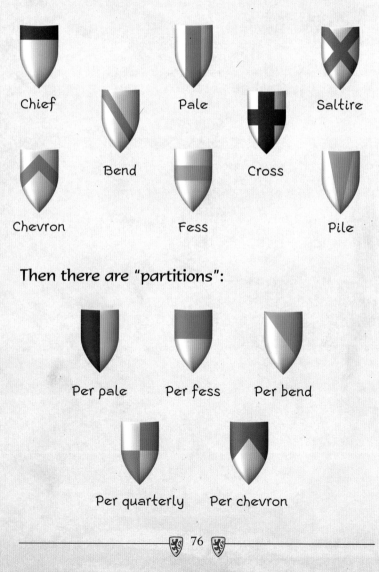

Chief

Pale

Saltire

Bend

Cross

Chevron

Fess

Pile

Then there are "partitions":

Per pale

Per fess

Per bend

Per quarterly

Per chevron

Then they get funky:

Paly

Barry wavy

Lozengy

Barry

Pale wavy

Bendy

Checky

Gyronny

You can even put a picture on your shield. Animals, monsters, fish, weapons, flowers – they all feature on coats of arms. Here are a few you might consider:

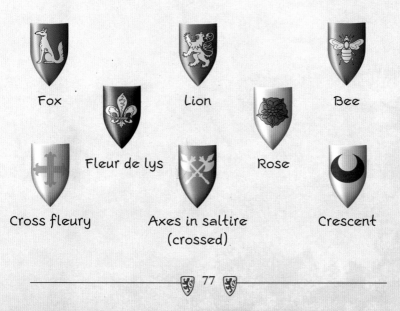

Fox

Lion

Bee

Fleur de lys

Rose

Cross fleury

Axes in saltire (crossed)

Crescent

Lots of knights have a picture which suggests what their name is. So if you're Sir Appleby, your shield might look like this:

If you're Sir Eagleton, you might consider this:

And if you're called Bottomley... well, you get the idea.

Good luck!

If you need any extra advice, you can contact the helpful heralds at the College of Arms in London. Visit www.usborne-quicklinks.com to find out more.